Publis...

This special volume of Charli... torn and chewed, by a Range... park. When the Ranger realised he'd discovered a brand new Charlie Small journal, he posted it straight to us and now *everyone* can enjoy this incredible adventure.

There must be other notebooks to find, so please keep your eyes peeled. If you do come across an amazing diary, or see an eight-year-old boy swinging through the trees, please let us know.

NAME: Charlie Small

ADDRESS: Near the Leopard Men's Lair

AGE: 400!

MOBILE: 07713 12...

SCHOOL: St Beckham's

THINGS I LIKE: My hover-scooter; Grip; Grapple; swinging through trees

THINGS I HATE: Leopard Men; Swords of Doom!

Charlie Small was here!

THE AMAZING ADVENTURES OF CHARLIE SMALL (400)

Special Notebook 1/2

Gorillas Vs The Leopard Men

BOOF!

Published by Pearson Education Limited, Edinburgh Gate, Harlow, Essex, CM20 2JE
Registered company number: 872828

www.pearsonschools.co.uk

Text © Charlie Small 2011

Designed by Bigtop
Original illustrations © Charlie Small
Illustrated by Charlie Small

The right of Charlie Small to be identified as author of this work has been asserted by him in accordance with the Copyright, Designs and Patents Act 1988.

First published 2011 by Pearson Education Limited

Based on The Amazing Adventures of Charlie Small series published in Great Britain by David Fickling Books, a division of Random House Children's Books, A Random House Company.

17 16 15
10 9 8 7 6 5

British Library Cataloguing in Publication Data
A catalogue record for this book is available from the British Library

ISBN 978 1 408 27401 9

Copyright notice
All rights reserved. No part of this publication may be reproduced in any form or by any means (including photocopying or storing it in any medium by electronic means and whether or not transiently or incidentally to some other use of this publication) without the written permission of the copyright owner, except in accordance with the provisions of the Copyright, Designs and Patents Act 1988 or under the terms of a licence issued by the Copyright Licensing Agency, Saffron House, 6–10 Kirby Street, London EC1N 8TS (www.cla.co.uk). Applications for the copyright owner's written permission should be addressed to the publisher.

Printed and bound in Malaysia (CTP-VVP)

Acknowledgements
We would like to thank the children and teachers of Bangor Central Integrated Primary School, NI; Bishop Henderson C of E Primary School, Somerset; Brookside Community Primary School, Somerset; Cheddington Combined School, Buckinghamshire; Cofton Primary School, Birmingham; Dair House Independent School, Buckinghamshire; Deal Parochial School, Kent; Newbold Riverside Primary School, Rugby and Windmill Primary School, Oxford for their invaluable help in the development and trialling of the Bug Club resources.

Every effort has been made to contact copyright holders of material reproduced in this book. Any omissions will be rectified in subsequent printings if notice is given to the publishers.

If you find this book, PLEASE look after it. This is the only true account of my remarkable adventures.

My name is Charlie Small and I am four hundred years old, but in all those long years, I have never grown up. Something happened when I was eight years old. Something I can't begin to understand. I went on a journey... and I'm still trying to find my way home. Now, although I've been attacked by ferocious feline foes, I still look like any eight-year-old boy you might pass in the street.

During my crazy adventures I've travelled in space, become king of gorillas, joined a gang of cut-throat pirates, and lots more. You may think this sounds fantastic. You could think it's a lie, but you would be wrong. Because EVERYTHING IN THIS BOOK IS TRUE. Believe this single fact and you can share the most incredible journey ever experienced.

Charlie Small

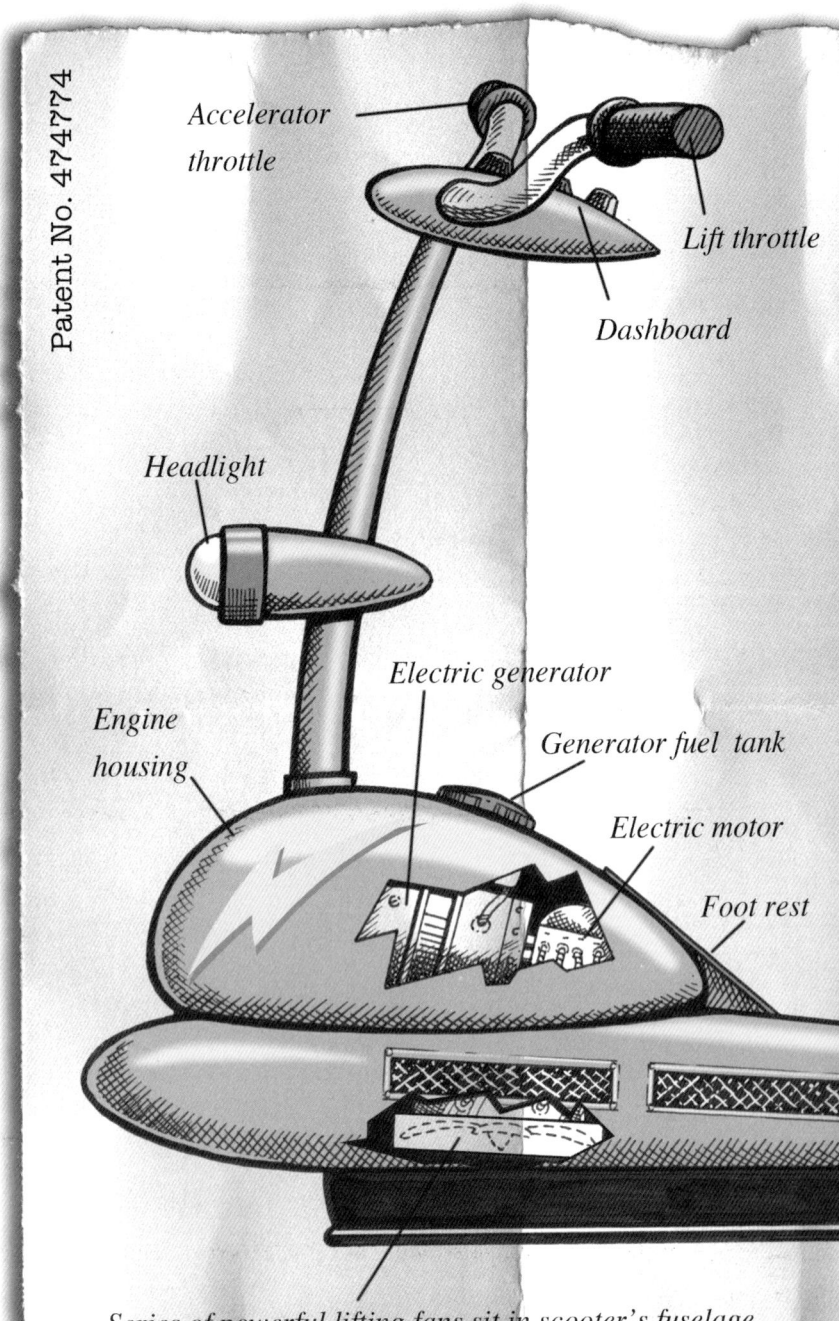

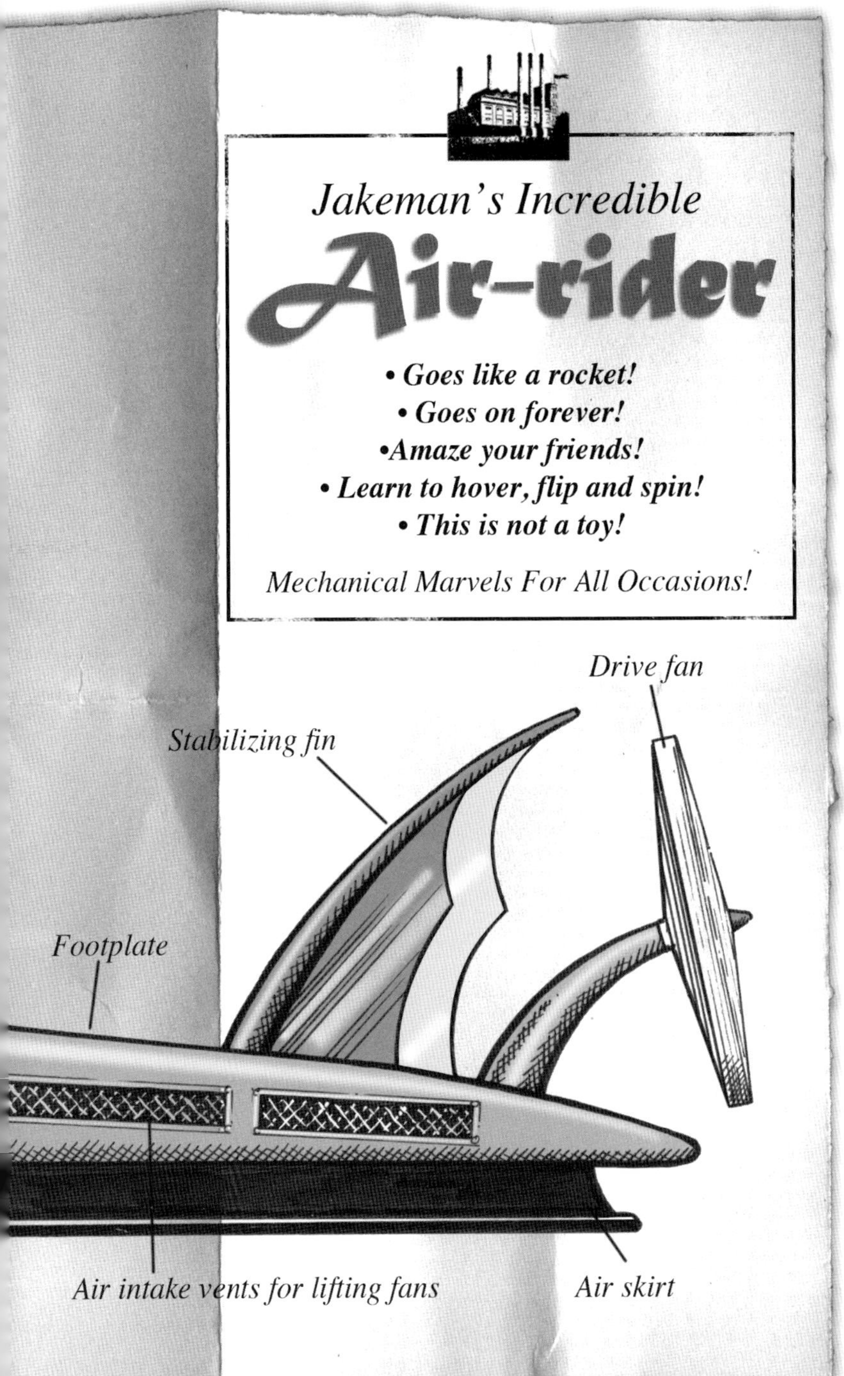

Jakeman's Incredible
Air-rider

- *Goes like a rocket!*
- *Goes on forever!*
- *Amaze your friends!*
- *Learn to hover, flip and spin!*
- *This is not a toy!*

Mechanical Marvels For All Occasions!

Drive fan

Stabilizing fin

Footplate

Air intake vents for lifting fans

Air skirt

A Rude Awakening!

I was driving across a wide plain on the Air-rider, an amazing hover-scooter specially designed for me by my pal, Jakeman. He's an incredible inventor whose marvellous machines have helped me loads of times on my adventures.

The hover-scooter hovered a few centimetres from the ground and I skimmed along at 30 kilometres an hour. The long grass rippled and the hot sun beat down, making the air shimmer and my eyes ache. I was in danger of getting heatstroke and I needed to get out of the sun.

Over to my left, the ground rose to form a series of low, cone-shaped hills covered with patchy woodland. Opening the scooter's throttle, I zoomed towards the trees and parked in their cool shade.

Suddenly, as I stepped from my scooter, a large flower sprang up towards me. It came up to my waist and its purple, rubbery petals opened like

The flower sprayed a powdery mist in my face. Yuk!

a fan and sprayed a powdery mist into my face.

I coughed and spluttered as more of the flowers rose up, filling the air with their strong perfume. I tried to weave my way through them but my head began to spin. My eyes closed and I gave a jaw-shaking yawn. I felt I must lie down. I just had to sleep.

Gradually, I became aware of a hand on my collar. I was lifted up, put under a rough, hairy arm and carried into the trees. The next thing I knew, a shower of icy-cold water splashed my face and a leathery hand gently slapped my cheeks.

"Wake up, Charlie," said a deep voice.

I opened my eyes and looked into the face of an adult male gorilla. His great head and short, thick neck stood on massive shoulders, and his arms were as thick as my waist and covered in coarse, black hair.

A Friend In Need

"Thrak?" I cried in alarm, thinking it was my old jungle enemy.

"Don't recognise me?" grunted the ape with a lopsided grin. "You, me and Grip play together, long time ago."

"It's Grapple!" I gasped. He was one of my two best friends from Gorilla City, where I'd become king of the gorillas and learned to speak their language. We had taken tree-climbing lessons together, and Grapple and Grip had helped me escape from the jungle.

"Wow, you've grown! You were a toddler the last time I saw you. Where's Grip?"

"Taken," said Grapple gravely.

"*Who* took him?" I asked.

"Grip and me look for new home. We out exploring when attacked by …" Here, the great, strong gorilla gulped and looked nervously around. "Leopard Men," he said. "They take Grip away. Please help, King Charlie."

"Poor Grip, of course I will. But what on earth are Leopard Men?" I asked, shuddering at the very sound of their name.

As my old pal gave me some banana fritters and banana bread from a small bag of woven grass, he told me about the dreaded Leopard Men. They are bloodthirsty carnivores, half-man and

Banana bread!

half-leopard, that roam the land in search of easy prey. They raid villages and camps, carrying off their captives to eat at special suppers.

"Where are they now and how many are there?" I asked, pushing my dinner to one side. I'd suddenly lost my appetite and was starting to wish I hadn't offered to help.

"Four of them. Very strong, very fierce. They camp on other side of hill," replied Grapple. "Got a plan, King Charlie?"

Yes, I thought. *Let's get out of here!* But I knew we couldn't leave poor Grip in the hands of the Leopard Men. I looked around for inspiration, and as I picked at the powdery mess left on my sleeve by the purple flowers, I suddenly had an idea.

As Grapple gobbled down the remains of the food and explained the layout of the Leopard Men's camp, I told him my plan. He furrowed his great brow and looked at me as if I were mad.

"Got any better ideas?" I asked. He hadn't and he knew he wasn't strong enough to overpower the Leopard Men on his own. So, with a sigh, he agreed to give my plan a go.

Will my plan work?

I'm four hundred years old – really!

Grapple has just beaten me at noughts and crosses!! (How embarrassing)

Phoning Home

In case my plan doesn't work and I end up as cat food, I've just phoned home on my mobile. Mum answered almost immediately.

"Oh, hello, darling, is everything all right?" she asked.

"Yes, Mum, everything's fine. I'm just about to rescue a gorilla from a pride of vicious Leopard Men. I might get eaten alive," I said.

"Sounds wonderful, dear," said Mum cheerily. "Oh, wait a minute, Charlie. Here's your dad just come in. Now remember, don't be late for tea, and if you're passing the shops on the way back, please pick up a carton of milk. Bye."

"Sure, Mum," I said as she hung up.

She says the same thing every time I call. Even though I've been gone for four hundred years, she's still expecting me home in time for tea!

Now my journal is up to date and it's time to meet the Leopard Men. I'm feeling as scared as a kitten – and now I'm not sure my plan will be any good at all. I'll write more later … I hope!

A Scaredy Cat

The Lair Of The Leopard Men

"Shush. Must be quiet," grunted Grapple as we swung from branch to branch through the trees. I hadn't travelled like this for ages and I'd forgotten how quick it is. Soon we were at the edge of the wood. We peered through the leaves at the grassy slope of one of the cone-shaped hills.

"We'll have to be extra careful now," I warned my gigantic friend. "Keep as low as you can and follow me."

I dropped from the tree and scampered across the open ground towards the top of the hill. Grapple followed close behind, breathing heavily. Just below the ridge of the hill, we squatted down in a shallow crater and I opened my rucksack and checked my explorer's kit. It was all there:

1) My multi-tooled penknife
2) A ball of string
3) A telescope
4) This journal
5) A pack of wild animal collector's cards (full of amazing animal facts)

6) A glass eye from a steam-powered rhinoceros
7) The compass and torch I found on the dried-out skeleton of a lost explorer
8) The tooth of a monstrous megashark
9) A magnifying glass
10) A long length of vine
11) My mobile phone with wind-up charger
12) A battered water bottle.

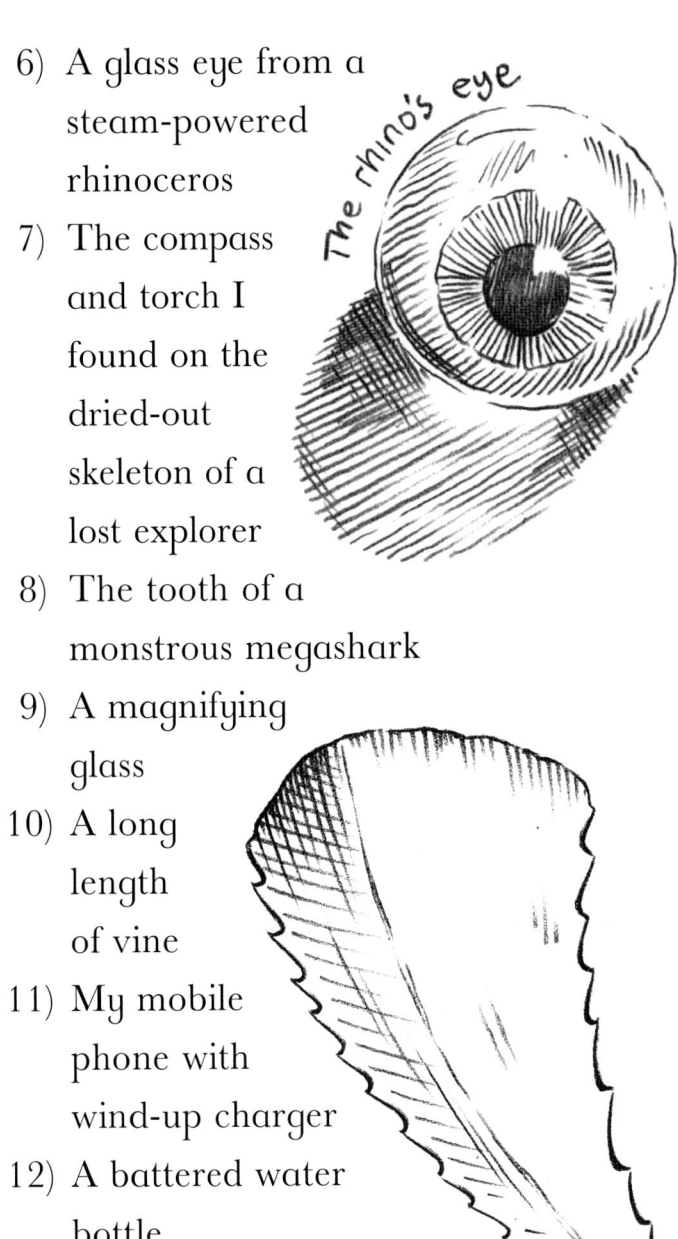

The rhino's eye

I'd collected some extra bits and bobs from Grapple's wood:

1) A long, hollow reed stem
2) A handful of vicious looking thorns
3) A small pouch I'd made from a leathery leaf and filled with the powdery pollen from the purple plants.

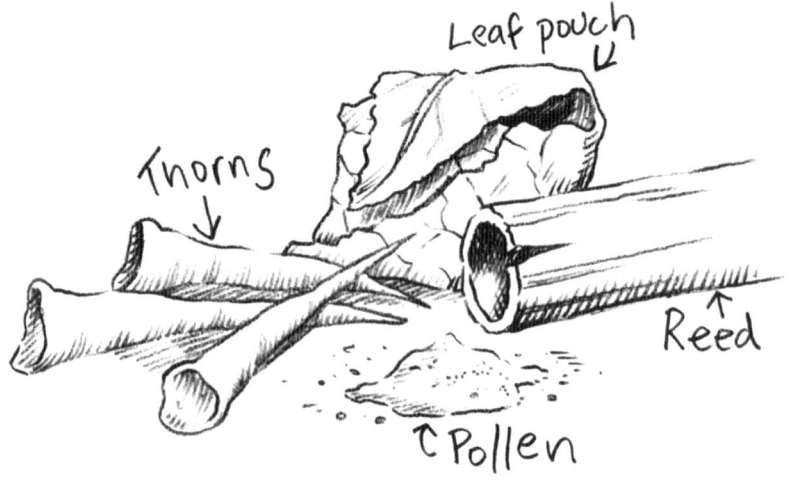

If these things didn't work, we were going to be in serious trouble!

We began to crawl forwards on our tummies. Suddenly, a terrible roar exploded and a thousand squawking birds rose in alarm.

I'm not easily scared but my legs became as weak as water and my heart thumped in my chest. Grapple gave a low growl of anger.

"They prepare special meal. Don't have much time," he whispered and slithered forward like a hairy snake. Crawling beside him, I peeped over the ridge.

In a deep hollow below us there was a U-shaped clump of trees. In the centre of the trees was a rocky clearing. A fire was burning on one side of the clearing and a raised block of stone stood in the middle. Tied to the block was poor Grip, straining uselessly at the vines tied tightly around him. I couldn't see his captors because of the overhanging branches. Then, with a hissing roar, one of the Leopard Men stepped into view and the hair on the back of my neck rose.

His muscular body was shaped like a man's but covered in thick golden fur and spotted with black. He stood upright like a man, his hands were shaped like a man's, but his head was one hundred percent leopard! He snarled, curling his lips and displaying a pair of enormous flesh-ripping fangs.

"Jeepers!" I whispered, realising just what we were up against. Then, gathering my wits, I said, "Come on, Grapple. Follow me."

A leopard man stepped into view.

Yuk! This bug got squashed between the pages of my journal. Don't touch, it might be poisonous!

Oh, Blow!

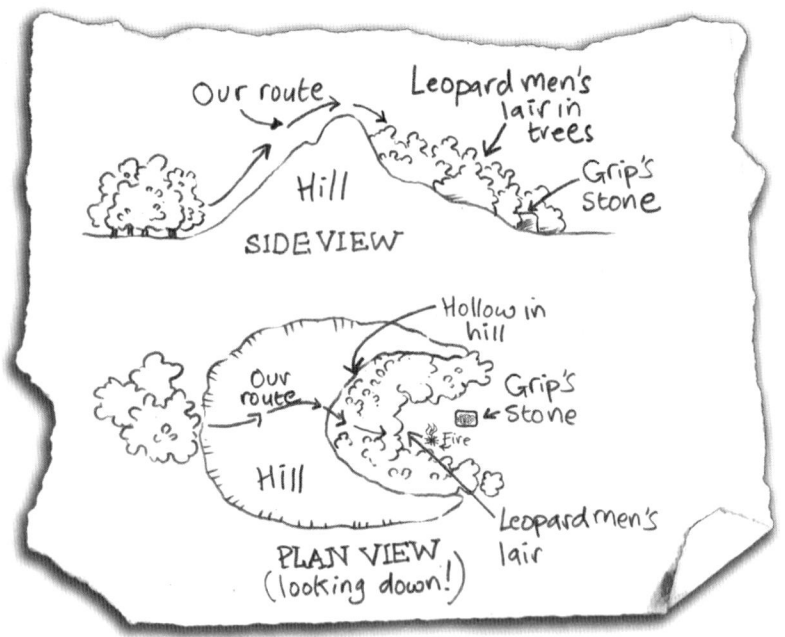

The ground on the other side of the hill dropped steeply into the hollow. The tops of the trees were just a metre or two below us. We skidded down the slope as quietly as we could and stepped into the treetops.

We moved noiselessly through the branches until we were perched high above the heads of the four Leopard Men as they stoked their fire and sharpened a long, flat sword on a rock.

"Sword of Doom," whispered Grapple in my ear. "It bring them power."

"You seem to know a lot about them," I said.

"Told stories of Leopard Men when youngster," explained my hairy pal.

Suddenly, with a horrible yowling, the Leopard Men walked towards Grip, one raising the sword high above his head. *Yeeeeoooowowow!*

"Bullying brutes!" growled Grapple under his breath, getting ready to leap onto the wailing cats.

"Whoa! Have you forgotten our plan?" I whispered. "Just wait a bit."

"Hurry or we be too late," said Grapple, becoming very agitated.

I took the length of vine from my explorer's kit, tied a loop in the end to make a lasso, and threw it over a nearby branch.

Then I got the big thorns and rubbed them into the powdery pollen I had collected. Next, slotting one of the thorns into the hollow reed, I got myself into position, raised the reed to my mouth, aimed – and blew!

The thorn shot silently from my blowpipe, ripped through the surrounding leaves and sank into the hindquarters of one of the Leopard Men.

BOOF!

Thorn

"Yeeow!" he yowled, dropping the Sword of Doom and spinning round. He took a few steps towards the bushes to investigate, but the powerful sleep-inducing pollen of the purple plant began to run through his veins. He stumbled – then, with a whine, he crumpled to the ground.

"Bullseye!" grunted Grapple.

I loaded my blowpipe again and fired off another dart. A second Leopard Man hissed and dropped into a deep sleep. The two remaining cats rushed around, parting bushes and roaring in anger as they tried to find their invisible enemy.

Boof! I fired a third shot and a third creature crumpled, but the remaining Leopard Man spotted us up in the branches. With a terrifying roar he leaped towards the trunk of our tree.

He Flies Through The Air With The Greatest Of Ease!

"Now!" I cried.

Grapple grabbed the vine lasso and leaped from the branch with me clinging to his back. With a blood-curdling yell, we swung from the tree like trapeze artists and Grapple hit the Leopard Man square in the tummy with his leathery feet. The creature was catapulted backwards and crashed to the ground, panting to catch his breath. Grapple ripped our lasso down from the tree and quickly tied up the stunned Leopard Man so tightly that he couldn't move.

"Yeow! I'll get you, you great, hairy brute!" hissed the Leopard Man, rolling around in a cocoon of rope.

"Yeah, right," scoffed Grapple.

"Well, that was easier than I thought," I said smugly – but I spoke too soon.

"Behind you!" yelled Grip, still tied to the stone. We spun round to see a *fifth* Leopard Man creeping towards us, stooping to pick up the Sword of Doom.

"I thought you said there were only four of 'em," I cried. "Can't you count?"

"Yeah!" cried an offended Grapple. "One, two, three, five, four. Like I said." Then, with a bellow, he charged towards the Leopard Man.

The big cat dived at Grapple, the Sword of Doom slicing through the air. They smashed into each other and fell to the ground, rolling over and over. The ape wound his massive arms around the Leopard Man and squeezed. With a wheezing gasp the Leopard Man dropped the sword but then managed to break free.

I stared in horror as the animals leaped at each other again and the air filled with roars and flying fur. Then, pulling myself together, I raised my blowpipe to shoot another dart – but I couldn't get a clear shot. It looked as though the Leopard Man was winning.

"Charlie! Over here," came a desperate cry. Of course, Grip! I snatched the shining Sword of Doom from between the

The animals leaped at each other again.

feet of the battling beasts and, running to the stone block, raised it high above my head. *Whoa!* It was much heavier than I thought and I couldn't hold it. Oh my goodness! The sword swept down towards Grip, its blade flashing in the dappled sunlight – and with a clash, sliced neatly through the vines that held him. *Phew!*

"Good shot, Charlie," grunted Grip, leaping from the stone.

"No problem," I answered shakily, dropping the heavy sword as Grip dashed off to join the fight.

Yikes! The sword was really heavy.

Grip leaped from the stone.

Between them, Grip and Grapple grabbed the frantic Leopard Man's arms and held him tight.

"Get him, Charlie!" yelled Grapple, as the Leopard Man broke free once again and turned on him with claws extended. I fumbled to load a thorn into my blowpipe. Then, shaking with fear and excitement, I aimed and fired.

The thorn stuck in the leopard man's shoulder.

Boof! The thorn whizzed through the air and, *thwack!* It stuck into the Leopard Man's shoulder, just as his terrible jaws were closing on Grapple's arm. With a huge sigh, like a deflating balloon, he slid to the ground.

"Phewee! Mighty close," gasped Grip, breathing hard.

"Too close," growled Grapple and, picking up the discarded sword, snapped it over his knee.

Grapple snapped the Sword of Doom in two.

"Yeeow!" snarled the only Leopard Man still awake, struggling against the vine that held him. "That sword is the source of all our power, you knucklehead!"

"Not any more," grunted Grip.

"Come on, you two," I cried. "Let's get out of here, before the other sleeping beauties wake up."

A Gorilla Hug!

It's a few hours later, and I'm sat on a tree stump, writing up this journal.

After retrieving my scooter, the gorillas and I rushed away as quickly as possible.

"I wonder if they are awake yet," I said, when we finally stopped for a breather.

"Will feel woozy," said Grapple with a

satisfied grin. "Was good shooting, Charlie."

"You bet," said Grip, tousling my hair.

"Oh, it was nothin'," I said, feeling chuffed. "It's time I carried on with my journey. What are you two going to do now?"

"We carry on look for new home," said Grip. "You help look. Stay and be our king again."

"I'd love to," I said, "but I promised Mum I'd be home in time for tea and I've already been gone for four hundred years!"

"So we say goodbye?" said Grapple.

"I guess so," I said. Then, in one swift movement, the massive gorilla swept me up in his arms and gave me an enormous rib-crushing hug.

"So long, Charlie," he said, blowing his warm, sweet gorilla breath in my face.

Grip nearly squeezed the life out of me!

"So – long!" I croaked. Then Grip took me in his arms and nearly squeezed the life out of me.

"OK, enough!" I gasped, and the big

beast put me back down. With a final wave the two gorillas loped away, and I looked around for somewhere to sit so I could write up my incredible adventure!

Where will my adventures take me next? I'll write more later!

This is
NOT
the end!

And that's
a promise,
Charlie Small

This is a Leopard Man's fang (actual size). I found it lying on the ground.

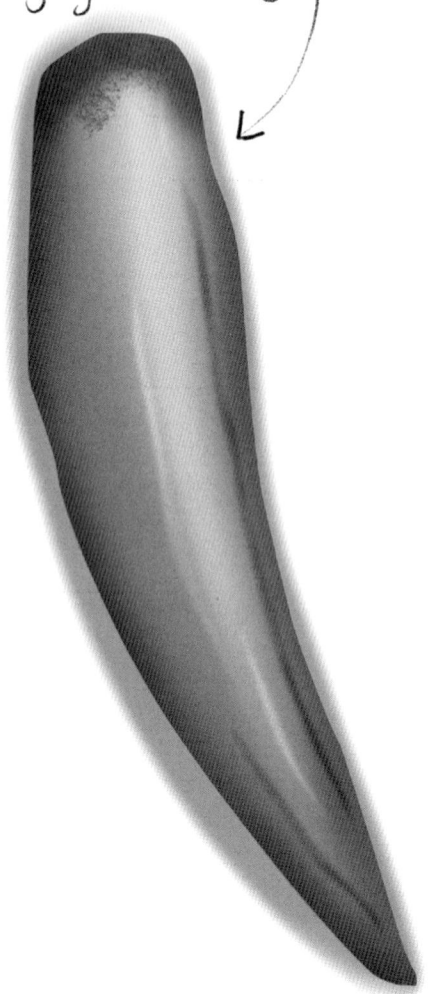

Woops. Missed a Page!

This is Bobo, the mean
mandrill monkey and
one of my worst enemies ever!

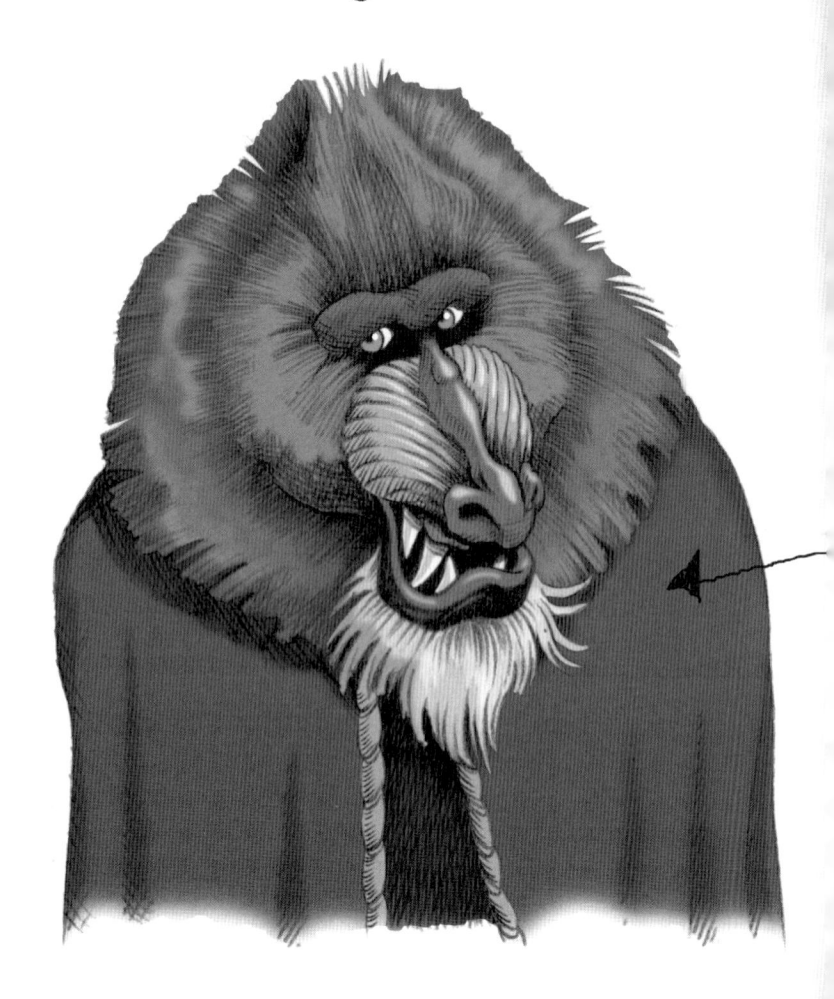

44

Latest chart!!

My worst enemies since starting on my adventures are (so far):

① The Leopard Men

② Thrak the gorilla

③ Joseph Craik - he never gives up!

④ Bobo

⑤ Captain Cut-throat

⑥ The Puppet Master.

Charlie Small was here!

Look out! Grrr! Leopard Men are spotty twits!

Grapple and Grip's autographs

(Grapple)

Gripe

Charlie Small
Charlie Small
Charlie Small

(Their writing hasn't improved!)

Grip as a nipper!

Grip and Grapple are my best friends ever.

Have you found one of my journals?

Which way is home?

My rucksack
Charlie Small
boy adventurer
Thrak is a great hairy twit!
PLANET
Joseph Craik is a wimp!